I AM ANIMA

Songs of Yin Energy

by
Honora Finkelstein

El Amarna Publishing

I Am Anima: Songs of Yin Energy

ISBN-13: 978-0615665344
ISBN-10: 0615665349

Printed in the United States of America

El Amarna Publishing
Grayville, IL
Visit our website at www.ElAmarnaPublishing.com

Dedication

To all my sisters who are learning about energy and empowerment, and to the animus inspired by all my beloved brothers.

I AM ANIMA

Songs of Yin Energy

Contents

I Am Anima

Das Ewig-Weibliche
Zieht uns hinan.
—Goethe, *Faust II*

I am anima
    unknown woman
        singer of songs in your nocturnal dreams
        echo of regret in your memory
    maiden mother
        my breasts ache with the milk of my love
I will satisfy you if you but ask
I will deny you nothing

I will deny you
    film of lace on flush of throat
    pearl drops of peach lobes
        untouchable
    la belle dame
    loathly damsel beckoning with gnarled fingers
    sibyl telling words you do not want to know

weaver of sensual tapestries I wait for your return
    the black rocks loom
    but still you see me not
        listen to my song—
        look back—
I am the face behind you, reflected in the water
        nothing?

            I WILL!
    come through the forest to my grotto
    penetrate the darkness with your flaming rod
        perhaps you may find me

I have a thousand faces
    but somewhere you have seen them all

I am anima
    singer of songs in your nocturnal dreams
    echo of regret in your memory

        where I lead
                you will follow

Honora Finkelstein

Truncation

You tell me to
"take it for what it is"...
Commitment is a concept you refuse.

How foolish some women are...
To think that "us" is always a part of "use."

Maiden's Dreams

Do I want a knight, fresh from dragon slaying,
Weapon rusted with the ruddy flakes of unwiped serpent's blood?
(I imagine the steaming wound,
Blistering bubblets dripping to the stones,
Incarnadined ooze, blotting scales that glister green and azure—
The monster curving-coiling-arching-falling,
A 7.8 shudder on the Richter scale.
Empurpled fleshly eye-ridges
Half-covering lapis-lazuli convexities
That saw the danger of the flashing sword too late.)

No! I'm sure I do not want an armored hero
Who makes his reputation wrecking reptiles.
Mind you, I'm not a bleeding heart for dragons,
Not like some of your craven border tourists
Who pity bulls and spurn the matadors.

It's just that those macho Hemingway conqueror types
Too often see a woman as adversary—
She is the prey and they are oh, so eager
To thrust their swords and draw a little blood.
"So what if it's maiden's blood," they say, "no matter.
A woman's not a woman 'til she's pricked."
Then off they go to fight another foe,
Or prick another maiden to the quick.
(I keep my eyes open for the flashing sword myself.)

Perhaps I cerebrate too much.
Perhaps I lack excitement.

But I'd really rather have a gentle plowman—
A visionary Piers who smells of sweat,
And soil, and fresh-cut grass, and summer apples.
A man who plows his fields with steady sameness,
Season on season nurturing pale green buds
To bring forth bread from earth and grapes for wine.

Though with the government subsidizing farmers not to plant,
I doubt there's any Piers around today.

Perhaps I'll settle for a CPA.

Honora Finkelstein

The Strawberry Handkerchief

Like Desdemona, to look, and looking pity, and pitying love.
Strumming the guitar like a minstrel,
    Singing of courtly love,
        Passion unrequited.

Children, playing in the street, get hit by cars.

The unnamed longing of a soul in anguish, crying out in your face.
It hurts to love.
    Is that what love is all about?
If I could hold your face in these small hands, I'd plead
    For your happiness.

Don't ever agonize again—know I have loved you
    With all the self-inflicted pain this simple soul
        Can grasp.

Can I bear to remember the lips—the gentle touch,
    Not asking, not taking, but for the first time
        Tenderly, gently giving?
        Because I needed.

What would Desdemona do in suburbia?
Yes, it hurts, by God—a dead-end street, with no house waiting.
    Perhaps, if things were otherwise, a string of rooms,
        But never home.
Fill me a parting glass, and sing me a ballad of loving.
In A minor, please, for it's a song of leaving.
Would you like to live two-hundred-fifty years?

To give it six months all its own, and say to it, this is real.
    This exists.
To enjoy it and know when it had faded, it would be
    Remembered fondly.

A fragile thing.

Could it live on? That would be true beauty.

Know this, then—you were wanted
    For an hour, a day, the time I had
        To spare.
I'll give you my strawberry handkerchief for your touch
    On my hand.

A very fragile thing.

Children shouldn't play in traffic.

Or with adults.

Am I as strong as I once thought?

I don't know.

But I'm alive.

Definition

Dilemma:

(noun)

a slimy horned creature,

generally nocturnal, which appears in

nightmares,

modern dramas,

and weary love affairs.

Hollowe'en

I touched your otherness again
And with it felt the weight of lonely being.
Sometimes it seems we are not separate.
But there are other times
When our two entities, though wrapped together,
Sever in consciousness
    Leaving a bloodless wound
    That suppurates in darkness.

A Fox in the Blouse

(From a Short-Term Mistress to a Short-Sighted Married Lover)

Your wife is having an affair,
though you don't know it, and I can't tell you.
    "You've done a lot for my ego, that's for sure!"
        My problem is I'm pathologically helpful.

But pity is a dangerous emotion.
    "Of course, all we can offer each other is the animal."
        And it wore thin from bouncing against your polaroids.

Red furry foxes. I know too damn much.
    "Isn't it odd? Most of the women who throw themselves at me
    are my wife's friends."
        Gnawing, gnawing.

Dull orange foxes, streaked with gray, I notice now.
    "I think my wife knows about us."
        If you could see through the lenses,
        you'd know it doesn't matter.

And busy little paws. I'd like to scream.
    "Do you suppose she minds?"
        Or throw up.

If you needed me, I'd take a knife in the bowels. But you don't.
    "She's pretty cool."
        I understand her.

            Go away, little man.

You took off your glasses to kiss me, but you shouldn't have.
    "Really, do you think my wife minds?"
        Nibbling, nibbling.

Take a furry animal and crush it
    By telling it the truth.
        Scrabbling, clawing.

Heroism is doing what one must.
    Politely.
        But damn! It hurts like hell to keep one's mouth shut.

            The streetcar named Desire is now a bus.

Honora Finkelstein

Emasculation Waltz

Perhaps it was too much booze.
        Usually is.

I squinted as his swarthy face blurred with closeness
  and his lips mashed mine.
      Please…I can't…breathe!

All systems had been go,
but we waited too long for the countdown,
  too numb from the drinks and the music and the smoke,
  I guess.
      It happens more often than we're willing to admit.
        More often than not.

Take off your glasses, lover.
      Ha, ha, joke
        He doesn't wear glasses.
        He DRINKS out of the them.

Eyes, unfocusing.
Hands and lips, touching the usual places.
  His and mine.
Fingers slipping down to massage
the chicken skin of flaccid flesh.
  Mine and his.

Numbness sometimes gets the better
of good breeding and politeness.
I can't feel…at all.
      But I'd never say *that*.

Your climax.
  My climax?
      Sis-boom-BAH…
        rah rah

Wherever did *ours* go?
Lost in the antediluvian period, no doubt.

Not quite…so rough…you don't want to kill
all sensation with too much pressure, do you?

Oh, CERTAINLY not. Good NIGHT!

What did I say? Why did you turn away?
No waltz again tonight.
    Put out the light.

Hand up to shield my eyes from the light
    and the smoke and the acrid stench,
I peered through the haze, looking again for a lover.
        I must have scrutinized too hard and scarred an ego.

Someday, a body will walk away.
        Mine or his, his or mine.

We're standing in a backwash of empty bottles
    and broken glasses.
        But as it laps with gentle slaps against my ankles,
        I barely feel the wetness anymore.

Honora Finkelstein

The Scent of Roses

(A few words on the process of individuation)

I keep the white flower of your affection on my breast
That its perfume may breathe throughout my dreams.
    No desiccated Lawrentian chrysanthemum,
    But a fragile mystic rose,
    Which, through some fragrant, vital alchemy
        Has never faded—
        Petals soft as the flesh of the belle I was…
        Odor mellow-sweet
        Synthesizable to an attar, but
            Unreproduceable

Perhaps it's your *blanchefleur* that's kept me jung and unafreud,
For Carl had sense in his surmise of women—
    Until I recognized the prince you are,
    Though it took years,
    I had no clear idea who *I* was.
And yet for years the rose remained my confidante,
    My inarticulate friend.
    Mandala for my meditative moods—
    Lavaliere of a love lost in the past,
        But found again at last.

At times you seem to evidence concern
That I'll be damaged by your strong desires—

    Ah, non, mon amour, tu n'es pas mon bête noire—
    Tu es mon bon ami, mon cher, mon prince…
        Mon bête!

Miranda's Song

You are both father and lover to me,
For you brought me through my psyche's tempest
    with cautious caressing.
And while the storm winds of my anguish were passing,
    you gave the healing touch that taught me
        not to fear,
            the kiss that woke me
        to a knowledge of unconditional loving.

Brother of my soul,
Preserver of my peace,
    You bear the rod of Aaron
    Though you may not be aware.

I love you with a love
    akin to adoration,
For through your love,
    I learned to love myself.

Now, looking at my reflected image in the waters finally stilled,
    I can say, because of you,
        "Ah, brave new creature, that has such worlds within."

The Jocasta Complex

A sad Stan Laurel face—
A joke, a Southern drawl
To hide the pain of being out of place.

And out of time again.
By life five decades past you've been beguiled.
You know the things my mother might have known—
Ramon Novarro, Coolidge, Al Capone--
The names that animate your conversation are common to old men.
And yet you're young enough to be my child.

You say your mother calls you Fanny Brice.
I've watched you play a femme role "just for fun."
You gentle, dear, and handsome-tragic boy-man—
I wish you were my lover…or my son.

Do Not Tender Me into Loving You

You are gentle
    and your eyes are soft with longing after twenty years rekindled.

It is easy to negate a Cassio,
    smug with his prowess marked by lipsticked handkerchiefs
    plucked fresh from maidenheads
    or cuckold's beds.
To such a one, who tries to shatter my resisting thoughts with
 seminal spray,
    drenching my hair in desire, I can say,
    "We were not meant for one another in this life,"
    and I can walk away.

But from you, who sit quietly by, watching and patiently waiting,
    I find it very hard to turn.
For though you yearn,
    you do not overwhelm.
You caress my wrist or touch my shoulder carefully,
    or brush a wisp of hair back from my cheek.

Of you I am afraid.

Do not tender me into loving you.
I am still a married woman,
    and I do not want to fall from Machu Picchu.

I do not want to live this life again
    four thousand years from now.

Pillow Talk

(A Gestalt Technique)

My guilty honest self admits
I do not want you back again.
At least, not the same you I sent away.

I cannot meditate on you
Or nurture our relationship—
Our breathing warmth's composted into clay.

And yet I write you letters
(Though on trivial, mundane matters)
And dutifully post them every day,

But from love's solar plexus
I have lost some vital nexus—
The granny-knot that bound us slipped astray.

You are charming-witty-bright,
Joking-clever, blarney-light,
"Simply wonderful at parties!" people say.

But the weakness of our linking
Is the fear I've felt you thinking,
That someday I may simply go…and stay.

For around you I must be
A singer only halfway free.
I must force my rimes to chime in with your song.

And in all the games we've played
I have often let you win
To keep peace, to soothe your pride—to get along.

But I'm I and you are you
And the axiom is true
That until one knows herself, she can't be strong.

So for now perhaps it's best
That we give our union rest—
To be other than we must be's simply…wrong.

For I sit here in the darkness
Talking to your empty pillow,
Feeling guilty for the warmth I can't recall,

And I find the one I've lied to's
Not the man I'm wedding tied to
But the woman in the mirror on the wall.

Honora Finkelstein

I Would Lie Down in Silence

I would lie down in silence
    if I could.

The television chatters in an adjoining room
Inane questions of Leno
    or Letterman
    or the strident urgency of some late Fonda movie
    (God knows which)
    to underscore the darkness where I lie
        by myself.

The sheets are cool against my heels and calves.
The rest of my body's bundled
    in the terry boxer robe
    you gave me last December twenty-fifth.
Not very feminine,
    but what I'd asked for.

Night after night
I seem to ask inane questions myself:
    "Are you staying up?
    Are you coming soon?"
I don't know why I ask.
The answers and the questionings have blurred.
    "Soon."
    A shrug and nod.
    And eventually you do.
    But never soon enough.

My pillow's wet.
I find I don't know why.
Oh, please, don't blame yourself.
For though I grieve,
    It's not for any cause I can perceive
        on your part.
And if, like some martyred saint,
    I burn, without the hope of a reprieve,
        I know it's the result of what I've asked for.

For you see,
    I have been guilty of a sin of omission.

I never made it clear that I was asking.

I'm tired.
    Of waiting for your interest.
    Of waiting for your love.
    Of waiting for you to turn the switch
        and end my jealousy
            of Leno
            or Letterman
            or Fonda
            (God knows which).

I would lie down in silence.

And alone.

Honora Finkelstein

Playing

we come together in a new game
but we bring each our old rules with us
and frustrations we have built in games with others
who made us conform in part to their rules as well

and so we have a catalogue
    of old game plans
    that do not…quite…fit
    the present situation
    (one cannot play "life" with "monopoly" pieces
    or win at "careers" with "clue" cards)

so often, though we try to play as partners,
we do so only tangentially:
trumping each other's aces…
expecting any moment that the other
    will respond
        as someone else did…
            once…
                in a different game

Eidolon

I cannot tell you what it is I need—
Not because I fear you would refuse it—
But because to name it
Would give teeth to its *raison d'etre*—

To make a thoughtform matter
Risks being ravaged by it—

Better to stand still—
Mutely dropping pebbles down the well of emptiness
And hoping there's no echo.

Honora Finkelstein

As a Woman Thinketh

You stroke my breasts and smile
    when to greet your touch my nipples rigid-rise.

You trace your tongue in crewel patterns down my belly,
    delighting as I arch my spine,
    and brace my heels,
    and lift my thighs.

You part my lips with gentle fingers,
    easing between them,
    and as I suck you into me,
    already nearly to the pitch of pleasure,
    you dilate with surprise.

And when together we have shared the waves
    of shuddering-precious lightning,
    you hold me still and savor all my sighs.

While I sit here, and you sit there,
    you do these things,
    though only with your eyes.

I sit here with a volume of Rousseau upon my lap,
    covering the pulse-beat heightened by the things
    you fantasize.

I look up…
    and you turn a page of Gibbon!
    Rapt somewhere in the Romans' fall or rise.

And I surmise:

The pleasure has been mine alone,
    the fantasy likewise.
    Mere mental masturbatory exercise.

Delicious lies!

Entr'acte

Over…
        and over…
                and over again…
You leave me.
        We seem to reenact the melodrama scene where
                girl loses boy.

I understand when actors play a role for many years
        they suffer burnout,
        the inability
to get a fresh perspective on the part.

It seems ironic, doesn't it,
after all the scripts in which
you left for angry, egocentric reasons,
that just this once you left because
you needed to fulfill an obligation?
        "I have to go away because…I love you."
Dramatic irony…
        and verbal irony…
                and certainly irony of situation.

And so once more I'm left on stage alone,
To perform a monologue, a *tour de force*,
And somehow…anyhow…I guess God knows how…
To get through the next act by myself,
While I wait patiently for your return.

I think I've played Griselda once too often.

Don't be surprised, my leading man,
If when you make your comeback to our playhouse,
You find
        the curtain down…
                the lights turned out…
                        the sets all struck…
                                the doting fans dispersed…

The ingénue gone on to character parts.

Honora Finkelstein

Umbilicus

The law said
    you were my husband…

But I thought of you as my oldest child.

I wish I hadn't coddled you
    or spoiled you.

You never grew.

Now the law says
    we no longer
    have a legal tie.
It's what I wanted.
I pursued it, in spite of you.
So…why
    Do I feel so sad?

Post-partum depression.

Hermetic Complexity

I thought your bedding me would heal—
bring benisons for wordwounds
and salves for bruises
I'd collected
from others' carelessness.
But your phallus—like a Swiss Army knife—
all tricks and gadgets and sharp edges—
no blessings there!
Just Anglo-Saxon striking.

I came away feeling sad for you.

Perhaps I had a healing after all.

Honora Finkelstein

Abishag

I would make love to you
I would with gentle lips and hands
    proffer you trembling pleasure.
        I would aggress—
        not repress—
    clothe you with warmth and then express
    the bounty of the flesh
    in measure full,
    replete with tenderness.

But the season is not right.

The autumn evening's chill
    defines the boundary that my blood may reach.
I must retain my warmth within
    until I know
    the consummation of the coming winter's snow.

If, when spring returns,
I find myself still here,
    ah, then, my dear,
    my beautiful one…

Then I would be thy Shulamite.

Ancient Battlefields

Perhaps we were soldiers together,

You a fierce captain,

And I your tenacious lieutenant.

Sometimes I sense in our power struggle

An urgency for victory distinctly male

On both our parts.

And in our love-making

Sometimes the grimace of brutality,

A need to mark submission,

A need to show who's field grade

And who isn't.

Yes, I think, my lover,

We have been before,

On other beds and battlefields.

And doubtless Greek.

Previously published in *SEARCH*, No. 1, 1992

Honora Finkelstein

Succubi

They're here again, those ghostly apparitions
　　From your past—
Scarlet-lipped, sloe-eyed, slim-hipped, open-thighed.

They watch me, and they smile—or do they leer?
Stonily laughing among themselves,
And whispering criticisms I can't hear.

Sometimes I cry in silence,
"Out! Avaunt!
Go find some other obsessee to haunt!"

And they retire…for a while…
To the shadows of my mind
Until a chance remark will make me fear the loss of you
　　To the memory of them,
And then I go and conjure them again.

How do I exorcise what isn't real?
How do I lay these thoughtforms
　　Of creatures who exist only for me?

Why do they terrify,
　　These phantoms of my mind
　　Of women I have never even met?
Because I fear they'll always be
　　As young and fair and lissome
　　As they were the nights you knew them,
While I, reality bound, with warts in evidence,
　　Will age, go up and down in weight,
　　And generally show my human nature.

I wonder if, to any other wife, *I* am a succubus?

Twin Flame

Beloved twin,

Whose flame was cast out into darkness
beside my flame,

Burn with me,
if only for a moment,

And help me be the light of the world.

Honora Finkelstein

The Seeker

I have sought you, my beloved, since the morning of the world.
Trembling with anticipation of what the flesh might teach.
In my Lemurian garden, fragrant with the mothers of hibiscus
    and honeysuckle and succulent horsemint,
I knelt in white raiment and watched the unicorns
    dancing in the valley
Until I heard you coming soft across the scented earth.
And I unlaced the sandals from your feet,
And bathed them with sweet oil of cloves and olives,
And dried them with the veil from my face.

I sought you, my beloved, on the steps of the Temple of Sriram.
With lyre and timbrel the procession of the faithful
Filled the air with vibrant tintinabular song.
You took my hand and joined me in the lighting of the sacred fire,
And clasped my fingers until noon had come.

I sought you, my beloved, by the waters of the Ganges,
Wet with the sacred river of desire, and cold in the afternoon's decline.
But when you came, recognizing me, and choosing me
    from among all the others,
You stroked the glistening droplets from my skin
And warmed me with the strength of your arm.

I sought you, my beloved, through the streets of Lebanon,
In fear the evening feast I had prepared would grow too cold to satisfy.
But when you came, gently parting the curtains of my tent,
We tasted only of the dates, and of the eggs of doves,
And of each other.

I sought you, my beloved, in the Arcadian glen,
And found you, waiting, as always, for me alone.
Under the boughs of the myrtle, silvered by the moon's full glow,
We lay together, and watched the progress of the pole star 'cross the sky.

And should this flesh be burned away
Through crematoria holocaust of atomic supernova,
And I find myself thrust once more
To the black and trackless vacuum of the universe,
Released to elemental aimlessness again—
I shall seek you, my beloved,
Through the times and worlds to come,
Through the waking and the sleeping
Of a Day and Night of Brahm.

About the Author

Honora Finkelstein has been an intelligence officer with the U.S. Navy, a small-press publisher, a technical writer, and a prize-winning features editor for Arundel Communications in Northern Virginia. She has been widely published in newspapers, magazines, and journals, has co-authored two nonfiction books, and has taught futurist and self-development workshops across the United States, in Canada, and in Europe. In the 1990s she produced and hosted a talk show on self-development and futurist topics called *Kaleidoscope for Tomorrow* on community cable television in Fairfax, Virginia, an experience that qualified her as an "agent provocateur."

Finkelstein was a workshop director for the International Women's Writing Guild for 15 years, has a Ph.D. in English, and has taught Western culture, literature, symbolism, and writing at several universities in the South, Southwest, and Midwest. In her teaching career she assisted over 30 of her students in winning local, state, regional, and national writing competitions and in getting their work published. She is the co-founder of Sunweavers, Inc., a nonprofit organization that assists writers, artists, and creative visionaries in getting their work out to the public.

Finkelstein is the author of two other books of poetry, *Kundalini Rising* and *Syzygy*; the metaphysical novel *Magicians*; and with Susan Smily has co-authored four other novels: three cozy mysteries in the Ariel Quigley series and the thriller *Walk-In*. She also assisted Smily in the realization of Powell Smily's 1970s novel, *Cross Currents*.

The Chef Who Died Sautéing won the Love Is Murder Readers' Choice Award (the Lovey) for Best First Novel, and was nominated for an Agatha Award that same year. *Walk-In* was a winner in the published fiction division of the Public Safety Writers Association competition, 2012.

To the embarrassment of some of her more traditional friends and academic colleagues, Finkelstein also does past-life and Tarot readings and occasionally talks to ghosts.

Other Books by the Author

Visit www.honorafinkelstein.com

Poetry:

I AM ANIMA: Songs of Yin Energy
Honora Finkelstein
El Amarna Publishing, July, 2012

KUNDALINI RISING: Songs of Power and Spirit
Honora Finkelstein
El Amarna Publishing, July, 2012

SYZYGY: Songs for Fools and Magicians
Honora Finkelstein
El Amarna Publishing, July, 2012

Available on Amazon as Paperbacks and eBooks

* * *

Magicians:
A Novel of Transformation and Co-Creation
Honora Finkelstein
El Amarna Publishing, October, 2011
Available on Amazon as a Paperback and eBook

* * *

The Ariel Quigley Mystery Series
(www.arielquigleymysteries.com)
by Honora Finkelstein and Susan Smily

The Chef Who Died Sautéing & A Killer Cookbook #1:
Recipes to Accompany "The Chef Who Died Sautéing"

The Lawyer Who Died Trying & A Killer Cookbook #2:
Recipes to Accompany "The Lawyer Who Died Trying"

The Reporter Who Died Probing & A Killer Cookbook #3:
Holiday Recipes to Accompany "The Reporter Who Died Probing"

Available on Amazon as Paperbacks and eBooks
Second Editions, El Amarna Publishing, April, 2012
Visit www.elamarnapublishing.com to learn more.

* * *

Cross-Currents
A Neo-Noir by Powell Smily
realized by Susan Smily and Honora Finkelstein
El Amarna Publishing, April, 2012
Available on Amazon as a Paperback and eBook

* * *

Walk-In
A Thriller by Honora Finkelstein and Susan Smily
Oak Tree Press, February, 2012
Available on Amazon as a Paperback and eBook

About El Amarna Publishing

El Amarna Publishing is dedicated to producing books, monographs, and e-books for an eclectic but discerning reading audience who enjoy the pursuit of leading edge ideas and philosophies.

We appreciate quality fiction and nonfiction of all genres. For example, we will consider publishing books on history or historical fiction; true detective stories or mysteries; science or science fiction; works on the American West or western novels; true ghost stories or paranormal fiction; women's literature or unique romantic fiction; and any other types of literature as long as the ideas presented are forward thinking and the writing is high quality.

We also plan to publish works of humor; unusual cookbooks; volumes on art, dance, drama, music, and poetry, as well as on the artists who create these things. We will promote well-researched approaches to mythology, symbolism, dreams, esoteric astrology, and divining, as well as metaphysics, mysticism, and magic; and we value the work of creative visionaries in all fields, especially in the categories of comparative religion, interfaith spirituality, personal growth, cultural history, humanistic psychology, and futurism.

Please visit our website for submission requirements: www.ElAmarnaPublishing.com.

www.ingramcontent.com/pod-product-compliance
Lightning Source LLC
LaVergne TN
LVHW051022080826
845145LV00009B/2757

* 9 7 8 0 6 1 5 6 6 5 3 4 4 *